I want to have a baby,

whatever it takes!

The tireless struggle against infertility

Carmen Martinez Jover

Acknowledgements

To my husband Sergio for his unconditional love and support, and to the light of my life, my daughter Nicole.

To my niece Gaby for sharing my maternal love.

To my family and friends, for always being by my side along the journey and, above all, to God and to life for each day and for everything which made me into who I am today.

Special thanks to Lone Hummelshoj and Christina Mackenzie for their help in translating this edition and to my sister Rosemary, for always being so enthusiastic in helping me.

Every event has a purpose
and every setback its lesson.
I have realized that failure, whether personal,
professional or even of a spiritual kind,
is essential to personal expansion.
It brings inner growth and
a whole host of psychic rewards.
Never regret your past.
Rather embrace it as the teacher that it is.

Robin S. Sharma

Index

Prologue

This book, which Carmen Martinez Jover had the courage to write, presents us with an unusual and unique mixture of images: chairs combined with coloured pencils, watercolours, rag dolls, butterflies and weeping willows provide a frame in which she expresses something that rarely manages to break through, one of those such profound feelings that produce a lump in your throat, of a pain that totally overcomes you, like the Peruvian poet, Cesar Vallejo put so well, "There are such powerful blows in life, I don't know."

And it is true: one really doesn't know anything, one understands nothing. Why could Carmen, who had played with dolls since she was a girl, not have children? Why did she have to go through so many treatments in vain? Why did she manage to become pregnant several times, awakening hope only to lose it each time? Why did she have to endure so much physical and emotional pain in order to get to know Nicole in the end? There is simply no answer, no one can either understand or explain it.

She herself didn't try to understand it, but simply tried to express in her paintings something which makes us all realise that as human beings we control nothing; that we can propose but not dispose, and that there are things beyond our understanding, because we never know what the future will bring. What Carmen's journey teaches us is that reality is as it is and not as we want it to be, and that we ourselves must adapt to it if we want to be happy.

This is the way it is and has always been, since we were a single cell. Like all living organisms we have had to adapt to our environment in order to survive, and to change our characteristics in order to achieve this, whether we are microbes, dragonflies, dogs, men or women. As Talmy Givon, linguist and anthropologist, expressed so well: "Survival and adaptation have always consisted of making intelligent decisions from the amount of information that the organism has available at any given moment."

To adapt is to accept, to have patience is to know how to read between the lines of the events and misfortunes that happen to us; adapting is knowing how to appreciate what we have and how not to suffer because of what we don't have, because when all is said and done, it is us - ourselves - who have made the unnecessary demands. Carmen wanted a biological child because she had been taught that this was what she had to do when she grew up, and because subsequently she believed, above everything, that this would make her happy.

But in the course of her journey she learned that nothing can make you happy except you, yourself, and that those who achieve happiness are those who live each day as if it were their last; those who learn to see the bad as a bringer of the good, who are happy and satisfied with what they have and don't miss what they can't have.

Carmen is profoundly honest in every line of this portrait, evoking sensations and feelings which many of us – both men and women – can identify with, and that many of us harbour in the very depths of our being, but which rarely come to the surface. As such, reading this book is a moving experience, and on the other hand it is also hopeful and beautiful as we see through the medium of her paintings an evolution, a growth of understanding, a transformation.

"After all," Carmen seems to want to say to us, "Why do we suffer so much? It's not worth it, because the sun will rise once again and we don't know what the future will bring us, we only have to face each day as it comes in order to be happy".

María del Pilar Montes de Oca Sicilia

Introduction

This book is a summary of what I had to live through in order to have a baby. During this *via crucis* of years of infertility treatments I came to understand life in another way and this has helped me to control the pain I felt inside.

On this path of suffering, painting allowed me to release my frustrations and defeated hopes, and it became a way of not sinking further into sadness. The paintings explain the history of my emotions, my ups and downs, my doubts, and the path to finding my inner self.

Over time I learned to change the focus of my greatest desire. The need to have a child had become an obsession but this suffering made me grow inwardly and value life from a different perspective.

I wrote in the first person as this is the story of my life, but really most of this experience was common to two people: my husband also suffered the effects of not being able to conceive a child.

I saw many doctors over the years and I hope this book helps them understand how much couples suffer during infertility treatments, giving them a glimpse of their feelings and helping them value their patients' time.

So much love

During my years of medical treatment I met many women who felt and suffered just as I did. There was a strong sense of bonding between us because we were in the same situation and we supported each other. That was how the idea of this book occurred to me. If the feelings of so many women are similar, and if talking to them helped me, I want this experience, which hurt me so much then, to help others now.

The aim of this book is to relate my journey so that my experiences can serve as a short cut for those who also have to tread this path of problems and difficulties in conceiving a child, as if it were a guidebook to make this route as pleasant as possible.

First you get married and
then you have a baby

First you get married and then you have a baby

Like every little girl, who plays with dolls, I believed that one day I would grow up, get married, have children and, like the end of a fairy tale, live happily ever after; but I never thought that the happy ending of this story would take so long to come.

Ever since I was little I always stood out as being extremely motherly. I loved to look after children and babies – even more than playing with children of my own age. I had hours of fun with them inventing all kinds of games, and was always the quickest volunteer to entertain them at parties. As a teenager I used to miss classes in order to go and help in the kindergarten when they were short of a teacher, and I have been the Godmother of many and named "aunt" by many more. It was because of my strong maternal instincts that infertility made me suffer so much when I couldn't get pregnant.

I was very much in love when I married and did not want children at first. I concentrated on achieving a solid marriage and financial stability. I used various contraceptive methods and after a number of years I felt the time for motherhood had come. I stopped using contraception, expecting to get pregnant any time. But the years went by and nothing happened.

My Wish

Afterwards I regretted having taken contraceptives. Why hadn't I checked with a doctor before to see if I was even fertile? But the thought I might not be had never even crossed my mind.

For me, the most natural thing in the world was to get married and have children. I had never questioned it, that was life, that was what I hoped for, one thing was supposed to naturally lead to the next.

I began to hide my feelings and this is how I started to paint. Art was a great way of letting go of the different emotions that were happening in the various stages of infertility. *My Wish* is the first painting I did. I wished that there was an extra place in addition to mine and my husband's at our table, a place in my life for a child, so that there would be three of us. That was how the idea of painting chairs originated, the chairs representing people. I never thought that from this moment onwards I would paint so many chairs, filled with so many emotions, which would help rid me of so much pain. When I painted this work I was still serene, I felt that at any moment my dearest wish would come true.

The candle represents my faith, the dove is God, and I hoped that one day, through Him, my baby would come. The chair at the end of the table represents the child I longed for, and the two chairs are my husband and I, waiting.

Waiting. This word is filled with so many memories and such despair. Waiting for so many dreams that didn't come true, waiting for results, waiting for the days to pass. I was always waiting, and time was slipping through my fingers.

My relationship with my husband was going better than ever, we were very united in our common desire. I was very much in love, and this gave me the hope to keep on seeking the baby I wanted so badly.

Our love was very intense, and I represented it as such in *Romancing on a Mat*. It was so passionate that the tile couldn't stand it, and fell off. But over time, passion declined, and it was now the doctor who would tell us the day on which we would have sexual relations.

Romancing on a Mat

This programming, which went on for so many years, cooled the spontaneity of the relationship, and it was not unusual that on the appointed day something happened, or we quarrelled, or we were just not in the mood. With time the spark was lost along the way.

We both had the same wish to be parents, but the need in me was greater. *Full moon* (pg.27) was painted after a beautiful evening in Cancun when you could feel the lunar power and admire its beauty. The full moon is radiating light of such strength that it absorbs you and leaves you gazing at it as if hypnotised. It was in this state that I begged of the universe, screaming into space: Help me, I want to have a baby. I had almost everything in my life, I couldn't complain of anything but my husband and I were united in our great yearning to be three.

Family and friends began to ask when the baby was coming, hinting that it was time now and that we were postponing it for too long. I would reply that we still hadn't decided when. I said it defensively because the truth was that we were trying but that nothing was happening. If I felt nauseous or had a stomach ache, talk immediately turned to a possible pregnancy and I reached the point when all comments made me uncomfortable. As the years went by the comments ceased because those close to us realised that something was wrong. They suffered in silence too, waiting for any opportunity to help me, but I shut them out.

I continued waiting for a pregnancy and after we'd been married for 10 years I finally began medical tests. I really waited too long to see an infertility specialist. I had never accepted that I might have a problem and I let too much time slip by.

After the first appointment with the gynecologist they discovered a cyst the size of a grapefruit, they operated, and I lost an ovary. There was a complication during the operation, the cyst burst and I had problems with endometriosis for several years afterwards. But despite this I was happy, because something had been found, a reason for my problems and by dealing with it I thought the path to motherhood was now clear.

It's curious how delighted one can be when they find things wrong with you. Now I laugh when I remember how happy I was that they had found a problem. When you come out of a series of tests and they tell you that nothing is wrong with you, it's tremendously depressing because you want something to be found so that it can be cured: this gives you more hope.

On this occasion, once I had come out of the operating theatre, and the ovary had been removed, I was put in the maternity ward of the hospital. When they were taking me to the room, the nurse innocently said to my husband: "Congratulations, sir, what was it?" "A cyst", he replied. The nurse felt terribly embarrassed, but it made me laugh. As I wandered up and down the corridor, making an effort to walk and recuperate, the doors of every room were decorated with "it's a boy" or "it's a girl", and my husband said: "I'll decorate our door with "It's a grapefruit" A cruel joke, perhaps, but it made me laugh despite wanting to cry so much. Actually, I feel that when a woman has had a surgical operation she should not be convalescing on the same ward as women who have given birth: it hurts.

Full Moon

Waiting

Waiting

"He who waits is driven to despair," so the saying appropriately goes. And I waited, and waited. I got to know many women during those endless afternoons or mornings in the gynecologist's waiting room. Hearing their stories made me feel better because many had problems which were far worse than mine, but still, one by one they each fell pregnant. I felt as though it were a lottery game and had enormous faith that one day I too would get the winning ticket.

It was a great relief speaking to the other patients knowing that I was not the only one having trouble conceiving. I had mixed emotions when someone had a baby: I was pleased for her but it was difficult to congratulate her because deep inside I was hurt as I wanted a baby too. Buying baby presents was a conflicting experience because I saw so many lovely things but got very upset that I could not buy them for myself, because I didn't have a child.

I saw pregnant women everywhere and they were beautiful. Wherever I went I saw babies. On street corners I saw the indigenous women with their babies wrapped in their traditional shawls, *Come along, son*. I saw so many children and thought how lucky the women were who had been blessed with the gift of motherhood. I thought there was nothing more beautiful in life. I want to be like that, I thought, it will be my turn soon, I felt that I had to be patient and hopeful.

Come along, son

I disliked Mothers' Day. "What a commercial day!" I said to myself, I found it so tasteless. Wherever I went there were posters, radio and television commercials. It was as if they were there to constantly remind me: *you are not a mother.*

The first two weeks of my menstrual cycle would pass quickly; I always thought this would be the month, this time it would be successful. After the hormones came the injections and following the doctor's instructions to the letter, and then the next two weeks were endless, everlasting. Every day dragged on for its full 24 hours, the week was interminable and as always the thought that I might possibly be pregnant made me wish those two weeks would speed on so that I could see if I needed to do a pregnancy test. I would notice that my nipples seemed a bit darker, my eyes a bit brighter and, of course, I always suffered from nausea. I had every symptom that I'd heard you got when you were pregnant. And then, huge disappointment, my menstrual cycle would start again and I just wanted to cry. I would cry the first day, but on the following I was ready and enthusiastically prepared for the next cycle: this time would be the right one. And the years slipped away in this fashion.

As the time passed I became obsessed about not being able to get pregnant. I cried much more but at the same time hid my feelings because I did not want to go on crying in front of my husband as the situation was now so repetitive. Not a month went by that I didn't think I was pregnant and then collapse in an ocean of tears. But my tears did not help release my frustration so it built up inside me like a pressure cooker.

I painted *Let go!* when I felt that I was locked into my own world. I had chained myself. I felt that however hard I tried I could not get to my baby. I had to learn to let go of the chain that bound me and made me feel so unhappy. It was as if I could really not move and would stay there waiting forever. I felt stranded. The wait had become endless.

My relationship with my husband was now one of helplessness. What could he do? Support my hopes of pregnancy and put up with my tears of failure. He

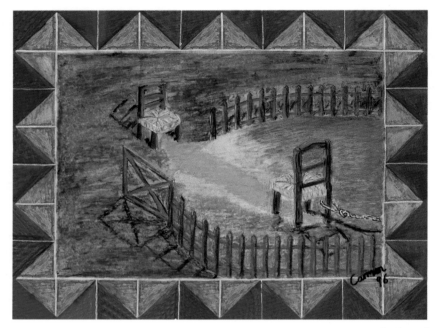

Let go!

suffered silently in order not to make me suffer more. He always seemed strong but I turned to my friends for support instead because I didn't want him to know how I really felt, emotionally devastated and sick and tired of waiting.

Medical Treatments

Medical Treatments

Medical treatments got increasingly intensive. Each time there were more injections and each time we wasted more money. After several laparoscopies and inseminations I remained un-pregnant. I began getting worried and changed doctors searching for the one who could solve my problem.

I had blind faith in every doctor I consulted. It was as though I rid myself of the problem by handing it over to him. It was a great relief, as though I was letting off some of the steam that was building up inside me. Now it was the doctor's problem and we'd see how he solved it. My relationship with some doctors was better than with others but now I know that each did the best he could.

I wanted to be able to see into the future, to see beyond the forest. I wanted to know *Which way?* was the shortest to my baby. I didn't want to make a mistake, take the wrong path and then just pass by the opportunity. I wanted to be able to predict the future to know which was the most direct road to my baby and shorten the wait. I loved having my Tarot cards read thinking that they could tell me my future and when they said I would have a child, or even two or three, I was happy.

By then I had lost my faith in medicine and was desperate. I needed to try other options but time was

Which Way?

running out: I was getting older and my chances slimmer. That was how I began looking into other methods. The information network among women is impressive: I heard that there was a magician in a market, a witchdoctor, massages which would warm your womb, a miraculous virgin: in a nutshell, any number of different options to

Come Closer

try and get pregnant. I went to many places, some I was impressed by and others not, but none of them helped me anyway.

Finally the moment came to try *in vitro* fertilisation (IVF). After finding out all about it, getting the right data, gathering the money together I went to the United States full of hope to undergo the first cycle of IVF. And finally it worked, I got pregnant, a pregnancy test was positive, I was full of hope, radiant, everyone around me was happy and I, above all, felt like the joyous princess at the summit of a mountain...and then I miscarried.

In *Come Closer,* there are the two of us, my husband and I, in our house, waiting. The baby is on its way, and beginning to climb the first few steps towards the nine months, but doesn't make it to the top. The baby doesn't complete the entire nine months of the pregnancy, and I longed, from the bottom of my heart, that the baby would please come closer and enter my life.

Once again I had suffered a loss, a loss of hope. I was in mourning, my fantasies and dreams of being a mother and able to enjoy having a child had been shattered. Moreover, I had spent a fortune on infertility treatments which didn't work. I was terribly disappointed. But, as was my habit, I gathered my strength, told myself that the past is past, let's move forwards and I began to prepare myself for another IVF. If the first had worked, even for only a few months – which for me represented an eternity - then the next had to be the one that worked. This was my motivation for doing another IVF: this one was sure to work.

I began speaking in my mind to this baby that I wanted. I thought about the world the baby's soul inhabited and tried to encourage it to come to me. *Welcome, come in,* I am waiting for you with open arms.

Welcome, Come In

As time passed, I became more and more obsessed. Being a person who had always achieved the professional goals that I had set for myself, it was difficult for me to accept that things were not under my control and that the final decision was not mine, however, I continued stubbornly in the belief that I would eventually get pregnant.

I felt that I had to continue and that whatever happened I would carry on, step by step, until I got what I wanted. *I will get there.* I would reach my goal, slowly, but I would get there, I was not going to stop, I carried on moving forward.

I'll Get There

How nice it is to walk along life with you was definitely true. My husband and I went through countless treatments, losses, sadness, hopes. All this was in the past, in the weeping willow. I like walking with him, looking for flowers and the good things in life and let's always continue to walk together.

Medical treatments are tough and shatter you emotionally. They either break a couple apart or solder them together. There is tremendous impotence because it is something that you have no control over. You don't like your partner to be sad, you don't want to depress him with your own suffering and so you begin to keep your feelings to yourself.

-44-

How nice it is to walk along life with you

A year later I had another IVF treatment, in Mexico City this time: once again the odious injections, the blood tests, the hours in the consulting room, the nerves, the waiting. This IVF also turned out positive. I was pregnant again and it was almost impossible to control my joy.

"Don't get your hopes up," the doctor said, "let's wait and see." There is a blood test called "beta" which tells you how the pregnancy is progressing. My attention was entirely focused on this blood test. It was done every third day and then I stayed glued to the phone waiting for the result. Finally the definitive result came through, and after two months of pregnancy I was informed that I had lost the baby once again.

Depression

Depression

"Don't get your hopes up too much", the doctor had told me, but how was I not going to be hopeful if the test had finally turned out positive? I didn't want to have a negative attitude towards my pregnancy and yet I wasn't supposed to have high hopes either; so I had to keep my emotions on hold, on pause.

When the doctor told me: "Well, madam, I am sorry to inform you that you're not pregnant after all", I can't tell you how long I cried for. I just wanted to cry and cry. I had lost that inner drive that characterised me. I had no desire to continue the struggle any longer. My strength had deserted me.

I painted *Another treatment?* crying. It was always out of focus as I painted because my eyes were full of tears. I thought I would never be able to go through another round of treatments. In the painting are the blood samples which they took from me, the rubber strap they tied around my arm when they took blood, all the injections I was given, the ultrasound equipment; but as I had gone through it all in such faith, I represented this with a cross. I hid the painting in a closet and every time I saw it I cried.

The injections had become unbearable. I thought I was never going to have the strength to go through another

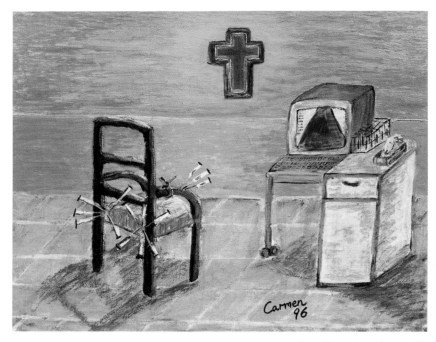

Another treatment?

treatment. Once again, I had spent a fortune and I was angry because all that money spent had been useless. I was annoyed with God, I didn't want to have anything to do with Him. I had lost my faith.

I fell into a deep depression. I didn't want to do anything. I felt that I was worthless as a woman. If my body couldn't bear children, then it had no use. I also felt that I was useless as a person, since I was incapable of giving. I felt that if I didn't get up the following morning nobody would notice. I felt a tremendous pain in my heart.

I Always Count On You

This is called depression, and eventually it all passes by, each person in their own time; but certainly there is always a way out and a lesson to be learned.

In *I Always Count On You*, my husband is helping me out of my depression. What did I learn? That things don't always work out as we want them to, but something better always comes along afterwards. When one door closes, a bigger one always opens.

If it were not by means of medical treatment, I didn't know how to get to my baby. It seemed impossible. In *How Do I Get There?* I didn't know what other path

How Do I Get There?

to take and the bridge had fallen down. The bridge full of illusions had collapsed. The sun, symbolising life, is smiling at me, as if to remind me there is always a solution to everything: one simply has to find it.

It is awful being depressed and touching rock bottom; everything was black and meaningless. I felt a great sense of loss, as though someone dear to me had died. What had died was my dream of being a mother and being able to give my overflowing love to a child.

My heart was broken and this was what motivated me to begin a search within myself.

The Search

The Search

My goal in life, up to this point, had been to have a baby. Nothing else was more important to me. I didn't appreciate anything, I took the good relationship I had with my husband for granted and the jobs I held simply kept my mind busy until my baby came.

I felt that an enormous emptiness had overcome me. I felt so unbalanced, so sad that I began searching inside myself.

I wanted to be in both spiritual and physical harmony, *All in harmony.* The chair represents the physical body and the spirit is a silhouette of a person. I felt that if only I could achieve this harmony I would get my baby.

I understood that in one's journey through life there are various goals: one is to have a baby, but that is not the sum total of one's life. I began seeking out things that I liked doing, things that fulfilled me. I could not see further than myself with a baby. Nothing interested me beyond that. Now, I had to find things that I liked doing.

I began to channel this overfill of love for children into my job as an English teacher. I went beyond the call of duty, I wanted to be a mother to all my students. Later,

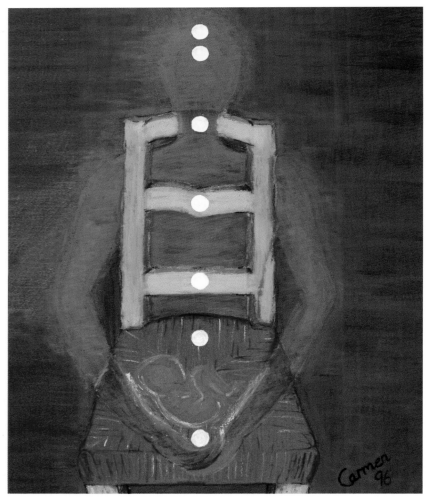

All in Harmony

I published a children's magazine in which I developed all the ideas I had of what I would do as a mother and what I could give to other children. My work as a teacher and the magazine were successful but I continued feeling

I Weep Inside

empty inside. It seemed that nothing could fill me.

Everything else in my life was going well, and nevertheless *I Weep Inside.* The flowers represent the beautiful things that were happening in my life and there were many of them. The hummingbirds represent the people who supported me, were by my side, but although everything was apparently going well, inside I was deeply sad because I could not have a child and this emptiness made me weep.

At first I was angry with God. If I was such a good person, why did He make me suffer so much? What was I doing wrong? Why was He treating me like this? Then I wondered if I had done something he was punishing me for. So, I made deals with Him and promised that from then on I would be even better so that he would reward me with a baby for my excellent behaviour.

This anger lasted a long time, I didn't even want to think about God. My friends would give me images of different saints and virgins, they would bring me holy water from sacred places, they brought me rosaries, gave me quartz and everyone prayed for me, except me.

What was the point? I saw no sense in praying as I felt that my prayers were not being heard. One day I came across an anonymous poem entitled "The Footprints", in which somebody is calling for God, asking where He is when one most needs Him and is told that he's being carried in His arms (see last chapter). This poem really touched my soul and made me begin to reflect about my life. I understood that life does not present you with challenges that you cannot meet and I understood, above all, that I was not alone.

Blessed Art Thou

I began to pray from my heart. I asked the Virgin to guide me, to help me, to give me peace and to give me what I wanted most in the world, a child.

Blessed art thou is a painting which made me feel very peaceful. I felt that someone was with me, but I understood that the answer did not lie in others praying for me, but that instead I had to open up, accept my situation and not wait for others to do what I had to do for myself.

I saw that sometimes situations hurt us and make us suffer greatly, but that we must always seek the way out. We should be constantly aware of the good things that surround us and understand that everything contains a perfect moment. When things are meant to go your way then everything flows towards what is best for you.

Yet Again

Yet Again

I never thought I would have the strength to undergo another IVF but nevertheless I did so. My husband and I agreed that this would be the third and last try. I think it is important to set limits. How many more are you going to do? How much longer are you going to try? If you don't set limits you just carry on and on. I know a woman who had 15 IVFs and none of them worked.

Happily I got pregnant again and once more had to put my emotions on hold. I regularly underwent the beta test and then suddenly: "Madam, this one did not work out well, but don't worry, we'll do it again just to make sure." While I was waiting for the results of this second test I knew inside that I had lost the baby yet again.

At this point I was *Waiting for a Miracle*. I represented it as an altar so that I could pray to everything at the same time. I knew that it was the last treatment I was going to undergo and I really was waiting for a miracle to happen.

The tiles represent the wheel of emotions: sometimes things go well, then they hurt you (the tiles which form a triangle), then you feel good again and then you are confused (the diagonal tiles), and this was the cycle of my faith. This was definitely not for me. The

Waiting for a Miracle

path I had chosen was one of suffering.

There's Still Time to Change

I had chosen the difficult road, one of stones and rocks which hurt me. But *There's Still Time to Change*. I had to accept that the treatments made me suffer a great deal although I always said that I was fine. It was as if I were walking blindfolded along the wrong path, but it's never too late to start over again. The curious thing about this painting, I noticed afterwards, is that the chair, the physical, is blindfolded, but not its shadow, the spiritual. It's as if you learn to listen to your inner voice in order to know which path to take.

I once went to an art exhibition and saw a painting with a chair, a road and a wall blocking this road. I felt as though I were that chair that had been struggling for years along the same road and had finally hit the wall. I cried when I saw that painting and realised that this nightmare of infertility was over for me.

The Lesson I Learned

The Lesson I Learned

I once had a boss who told me that in every crisis there are hidden opportunities. I never forgot this piece of advice. Great opportunities very often arise from desperate situations, one simply has to be able to recognise them. Often, when you are going through a difficult period and see everything in black, it is important to stand back to see what you have actually achieved as a result of not having what you think you want, and you will be surprised.

The truth is that if I had had a child years ago I would never have painted, I would never have been a teacher, nor would I have had the same enthusiasm to help as many children as I did.

You have to flow through life. In this painting, *Flow!,* there is a weeping willow which represents a difficulty: we can't avoid it, and sooner or later it must be faced. You have to flow, and have faith in yourself and that, in the end, everything that happens is for the best. I feel that when you are on the right path everything flows more smoothly and doors open up. Have faith and follow the light at the end of the river. This light will guide you – it is your heart and you must learn to listen to it.

Flow!

I had to accept my problems, live with them and seek out happiness in order to find fulfillment. I thought that my only happiness was in having a baby, and I was completely wrong. There are many things, people, and events, which can give you happiness and fill your heart with love. You simply have to open yourself towards them.

There is always a nephew, niece or Godchild that can help you to get out all you have to give. Even a pet is an excellent way of sharing this emptiness, then they are so spoilt that they don't know they are animals.

These children around us can share many lovely moments and soothe the desolation of not being a mother.

I came to understand that you have to seek your happiness now, with every opportunity that life gives you. Live and enjoy today, tomorrow will bring other joys. Today is the best day of your life and you have to enjoy it to the maximum. It's important to find that happiness today.

Adoption

Adoption

I needed to examine whether I really wanted to be a mother or if it was just life's inertia that made me think that that's what I wanted. Society expects children to follow on after marriage. I had spent years trying to get pregnant, I now had to decide if I really wanted a child or if the desire had simply become a habit after so many years of trying.

This is what was going through my mind when I painted *Playing mother.* Was it like a child's game that you want to keep on playing, or do you really want to be a mother? I really started considering this point when I began to think about adoption.

As it is always important to keep walking through life, I couldn't stop at the junction. In *Choose!* I was afraid of making the decision to adopt, and wanted to stay there, immobile, as if hoping that some miracle might happen. But I had to choose to take either the left or the right path. It was a very difficult decision to take. But I understood that life goes on and choices have to be made; you can't stay paralysed by indecision.

I concluded that deep down I did really want to be a mother, that I had a lot to give and that thus adoption was a real option for me.

Playing Mother

There are people who feel very stable as a couple and who come to the conclusion that they have no need to have a child. Their lives are complete without children and they have found their happiness this way. Those who decide that they do want to have children begin to investigate the possibilities of adoption.

I was frightened of adopting because I knew nothing about it. There are many uncertainties regarding adoption: will I love the child? Will we bond? Will we get along? Will we adapt to a child? What about its unknown genes? Will our families accept the child? And what about the child's background? These types of questions arose because I had no information, and doubts were raised in my mind which made me delay and put the final decision off.

So I started looking into it. How I would have liked to have had more information on adoption earlier! Once I had taken the decision I thought everything would be smooth as silk and I would have my baby in a question of days. Imagine my surprise when I discovered there was a two-year waiting list and an age limit. I was 39, I had hit the limit and I was considered too old to adopt. This came as a real shock. So many years of trying to get pregnant and now that I had finally decided to adopt, I was too old. How could it be that in all my life no one had ever told me this?

The next step in the process of adoption is to gather together all the documents you need to submit. I nearly died when I saw the list! The amount of paperwork is interminable. Of course, now I understand that handing over a baby is a very serious matter and those responsible

Choose!

have to make sure of the kind of home it will have. At the very beginning I thought that it was going to be difficult to get everything that was required.

I was applying through four adoption agencies, so prepared four packets of documents. I was very nervous at all the interviews, I wanted to prove that I was an excellent wife, daughter, sister, daughter-in-law, everything. I was afraid that something would stop them from giving me a child. I wanted to highlight my virtues and hide my defects.

I was so nervous during the psychological tests: I thought they may misinterpret a drawing and for that reason would not let me have a baby. I was very tense during this adoption procedure. I took a course for adoptive parents as it is always helpful to meet others in the same situation. It is important not to get tense and anxious, one has to relax, get on with the proceedings and interviews without getting overwhelmed because at the end of the road, you will get your child. I found the whole legal process of adoption agonising but it was worth being patient.

Unlike problems of infertility, I knew that by going through the procedure I would sooner or later get a baby and it was just a question of waiting. Once again, waiting.

In the painting *The Wait* I am holding my arms open, just about to welcome my baby; I still have to wait a little longer but she is now much closer, I almost have her.

Before adopting you go through a period of mourning for the biological child you will never have, but you must also prepare yourself emotionally for the adopted one you will have with all the joys that that entails.

In Mexico there are two types of adoption: full and simple. I advise full adoption which gives you all legal rights over your child and many other benefits. And I urge you to always tread the legal path: it is common to hear of someone who doesn't want her baby or of an abandoned infant. One is so desperate to be a mother that it is easy to be tempted, but always go to the formal adoption agencies, who are always ready to inform and help you.

The Wait

Life gave me the opportunity to adopt a baby that had been born with respiratory problems. He had gone through his first week of life in intensive care, and when he was moved to medium therapy they asked me if I wanted him. He weighed just two pounds, and appeared to be the result of an unwanted pregnancy. He had sores all over his body and he was connected by tubes to all kinds of monitors. I spent a whole week with him in the hospital. I sang to him, spoke to him, hugged him and he began to breathe more easily, and the most beautiful thing was that he smiled when he heard my voice. But, in the mysterious ways of life, he didn't manage to survive, and died when he was only two weeks old. His death hurt me deeply, but I think that in his two weeks of life he was happy, and he died with a smile. This was an exceptional case; normally they approach you when the baby's papers are already in order and they are ready to go home with you. But in this case the child needed love and I had accepted the risk.

I was inconsolable so my husband took me to Miami on holiday. A week later we got a phone call at the hotel to say that our daughter had arrived, that she was two months old and was waiting for us. Deep down inside I think the baby boy who died was a little angel who brought me my daughter. Nicole came to us within a year of waiting, a gift of life.

We spent two long sleepless nights. The day we went to pick her up, we went into a room by ourselves where she lay in a small beautiful cradle. We grasped our hands, our hearts were beating rapidly as we approached the cradle.

When we moved the lace curtain back to see her for the first time, she smiled at us, the most beautiful smile I have ever seen in my life. It was as if she wanted to say: "Well, it's about time you got here! I've been waiting for you." We shed tears of happiness. We picked her up and hugged her without being able to contain our tears of joy. It was love at first sight. We have loved her intensely from the very first moment that life presented her to us.

I had finally reached my goal at the end of a very long journey, and after years of treatment, suffering and hopes here were *The three of us*.

We adopted our daughter, Nicole. She is an angel that came to our home. She has filled our lives with blessings. So much is the love and happiness that it overflows from within, from the very depths of our soul.

I have not told you my story to convince you to adopt because everyone has to find their own solutions. But what I do want to say is that there is an answer to everything in this life. We simply have to decide what we want.

The Three of Us

Five Years Later

Five Years Later

So here we are, the three of us, living a normal life with its ups and downs, just like any other family. I continue to paint, although my work has changed a lot. I am no longer painting chairs, they have been left behind.

Nicole is five years old now. She is a beautiful, intelligent, happy and confident child. I forget that she is adopted and although she is still too young to fully understand this when she is old enough to understand she will have always known. I was born on the 2nd July and she on the 3rd of the same month. This cannot just be a coincidence: we were obviously meant for each other.

All the pressure was released from the relationship with my husband and everything we had gone through has been put behind us. I became pregnant twice more during this period but miscarried after three months both times, so decided to have my fallopian tubes tied. It may sound illogical to have my tubes tied if I'd never been able to give birth, but now, at the age of 45, I am a happy woman and mother; my life is full, complete.

Now I really enjoy Mother's Day, particularly when my daughter gives me a bunch of flowers and says "I love you, Mummy."

I welcome listening to women who are living the same situations as I did. I hope that when talking to me, they see themselves reflected in my experiences as I see myself reflected in their tears. Hoping that with this they can regain their inner peace and have strength to continue.

I thank life, for every moment, for all my experiences and the lessons learned and accept my past as the teacher that it is.

Other paintings

Other paintings

There are some other paintings related to infertility that I would like to share with you: the first two are exhibited in an infertility treatment clinic.

Magical Dawn

This painting *Magical dawn*, uses symbols to express the magical dawn of a new human. The spiral and the stars are the universe. How many more discoveries might there be in the immensity of the universe? The chair is the doctor, the bees are people who, like him, work hard. The bee buzzes from flower to flower carrying pollen and fertilising each plant, and there are nine little souls waiting for the moment to fertilise the cell and become a child.

Magical Birth

Magical Birth describes the process from conception to the birth of a baby. The sun represents an egg with spermatozoa, and just as any plant grows, so does a baby, dividing into nine parts like the nine months of gestation. There is something magical about the way two cells come together to form a human being. But both before and after there is a celestial aura, which is the divine aspect. No matter how advanced science becomes, God is always present.

This painting, *Bosco's Tree of Life* is important to me because it is the first in which I expressed fertility as something beautiful. I had my daughter when I did it and saw life in a different light.

Bosco's Tree of Life

It is a family with nine children, fertility in abundance, a tree of life.

There is another painting which is very special to me, related to life and death. It tells the story of a seriously ill nine year-old girl. Her last wish was to collect frogs. When I asked her "why frogs?", I was told that her father had always sung to her: "heal, heal, frog's tail, if you don't get better today you will tomorrow." We sing this little ditty in Mexico when a child has hurt itself. This was moving, for what she wanted was health, life.

I represented the girl as a chair set on lily pads; these can either keep her afloat or let her sink. In the background are two waterfalls which merge: the mother and father united so that the water in the pond stays as still as possible, making the girl's last days as loving as they can, but they have no control over the lily pads. A frog sits on the chair giving orders to the others, some of which are waiting, while one pushes a lily pad and another is jumping trying to place another lily. The frogs represent the girl's faith that she will continue living. Miraculously to this day her inner strength continues to maintain the lily pads under her feet.

I hope this book will be a sort of *"heal, heal frog's tail,"* which will help heal your wounds and draw out your inner strength guiding you towards inner happiness.

Heal, heal frog's tail

About Myself

About Myself

I love painting: it is my space, my hiding place, my precious moments of solitude, of time to myself.

I've loved art since I was a teenager. At school I had a Scottish teacher who encouraged me to paint and taught me the art of *batik*, a technique which involves wax and water-based dyes.

I used to paint for pleasure, when I had to give a present, or to decorate a wall in my house. When I painted the first picture of chairs, *My Wish*, it was just because I wanted a painting for the dining room. I thought that chairs were an appropriate theme, and it complemented the room. In the beginning, I used to paint one picture each year. As the years passed, I painted more pictures of chairs in order to express my feelings. I never imagined that I would eventually become a professional painter. With time, painting came to serve as my means of escape. It was easy to project my personal feelings onto the canvas.

I had painted several pictures. At that time I used to teach English classes in a school near my house, and I decided to take a portfolio of my work to school to offer them for sale. I really liked some of the paintings, however, and didn't want to sell them, so I labelled them as my *'private collection'*. One of the teachers was captivated by one painting entitled *How Nice It Is To Walk Through Life With You*, which happened to be in my private collection. I didn't want to sell it; it felt like I would lose a part of myself. The painting represented my love for my husband and our difficult moments in the past. I wanted to have it with me always. When I told my husband about it, he said: "Our love exists with or without the paintings. If you want to be an artist, you have to learn to let go of your paintings."

The next day, I spoke to the teacher and took the picture to her. I was holding the picture in my right hand and she took it with her left. For a moment I held on to it, and during that split second I thought that I could still change my mind. Then I let go, hugged her, and we cried, and she promised to take very good care of the painting, as she too valued it highly. That's how I delivered my first paintings and began selling little pieces of myself. I have continued to do so ever since.

As I painted, I grew attached to each work of art, it felt as if each one of them was a little child of mine. I still feel very happy when I see them again, for each one tells its own story and stirs emotions in a unique way.

I really liked a picture by Jan Van Dyck titled *Portrait of Arnolfini and His Wife,* because it is filled with symbols: everything in the picture has a meaning. I have also loved the way that Frida Kahlo expressed with such power the emotions she was living. In distinct ways these two artists have had a great influence upon my painting.

One morning, another teacher came to me and said that she wanted me to paint her. I was a little taken aback, surprised at first, as I was only used to painting chairs. She explained to me that since I painted feelings with chairs, she wanted me to interview her and her family so I could paint them in the same way. That's how I painted my first portrait of a family. Who would have imagined that with this suggestion she would provide the impetus to painting so many more portraits after that.

I loved speaking with families, listening to them tell me their histories, what they had lived through, their anecdotes, and afterwards being able to capture it on canvas. Whenever I delivered a painting, actually handing it over, was always a very emotional experience, as each one was filled with very unique and personal symbols customized for the person who had commissioned it. What was most important to me was that the picture touched the heart of the person who appeared in the work. And so for many years I painted portraits to order. They were very beautiful years, each picture had its own charm, and the experience of painting them was very satisfying.

On one particular occasion, one of my students decided to interview me for his homework. His assignment was to interview a well-known artist, and he thought of me. This was my very first interview. He arrived with his two brothers, one was the cameraman and the other the assistant. He came very well prepared with questions to ask. Afterwards he gave me a copy of the video, which I still have and cherish. These three children, were in my English classes for many years and, at the time they filled the emptiness that I felt because of not having children. They occupy an important place in my heart.

A doctor who was moved by my paintings on the theme of infertility was organising a symposium and invited me, as he felt that it was important for doctors to understand their patients' emotional experiences. After that, I attended a number of symposia and many women approached me and began to cry, as they identified with the experiences depicted in the paintings. The doctors were also moved.

I also took part in a bioethics congress where a psychologist analysed my pictures. I have given talks in high schools, emphasising that one should be authentic, not be afraid, and flow with life. The important thing is to stimulate creativity in all fields and raise the self-esteem of students.

Through those coincidences in life, I came into contact with a gallery in Miami, which has since promoted my work at an international level. My work has appeared in books, magazines and newspapers. One thing has lead to another.

When I first had my daughter I painted very little; in those early years I must have painted only about five pictures. I devoted my time to her, and painted only in the few spare moments I had. But when Nicole started kindergarten I took up painting again in the mornings. To this day, I continue to paint while she is at school.

I no longer felt an urge to paint chairs, but I didn't know what else to paint; I wanted to close that stage of my life, but I also felt intimately bound to the chairs. I thought that leaving them behind would be like starting over again and perhaps losing what I had achieved. But because I also felt that it was important for me to be true to myself, I left the chairs behind and painted angels instead. In that way, too, I managed to touch the hearts of people who saw the paintings and were moved by them.

After the period of angels I went through a creative block, I didn't know what to paint. I felt totally and absolutely lost. I began to take art classes and to try out new techniques and to find what felt right.

For several years now I have felt the need to publish this book, but other things have claimed my attention and, without realising it, the book kept getting postponed. I feel it is important to share these experiences, so that my readers can identify with them, and know that they are not alone. After many years I can finally close this chapter of my life.

I am currently preparing an individual exhibition with an Indian theme. I get up full of energy every day, leave my little girl at school, and spend the whole morning painting. Painting fills my soul, it is my way of capturing and expressing the feelings I have inside. I paint in a lovely studio which looks onto a garden filled with trees and flowers. All morning I am surrounded by birds and their enchanting song. Whatever may become of my painting, I don't know. I simply enjoy the moment; I enjoy the now and paint from the heart.

Footprints

(Basada en una alegoría anónima)

One night I dreamed I was walking along the beach with the Lord. Many scenes from my life flashed across the sky.

In each scene I noticed footprints in the sand. Sometimes there were two sets of footprints, other times there was one only.

This bothered me because I noticed that during the low periods of my life, when I was suffering from anguish, sorrow or defeat, I could see only one set of footprints, so I said to the Lord,

"You promised me Lord, that if I followed you, you would walk with me always. But I have noticed that during the most trying periods of my life there has only been one set of footprints in the sand. Why, when I needed you most, have you not been there for me?"

The Lord replied, "The years when you have seen only one set of footprints, my child, is when I carried you."